Why We Are in Need of Tails

Why We Are in Need of Tails

Story by Maria daVenza Tillmanns

Illustrations by Blair Thornley

IGUANA

Published by Iguana Books
720 Bathurst Street, Suite 303
Toronto, ON M5S 2R4

Publisher: Meghan Behse
Editor: Holly Warren

ISBN 978-1-77180-390-8 (hardcover)
ISBN 978-1-77180-372-4 (paperback)
ISBN 978-1-77180-373-1 (epub)
ISBN 978-1-77180-374-8 (Kindle)

This is an original print edition of *Why We Are in Need of Tails*.

To Mr. Lizzard

Fairy Tails

Once upon a time, before we had fairy tales, we had actual tails. Everyone had them.

Everyone had them.

It made sense. Tails connected us to the world and to others and wove us into the fabric of life.

We had long tails, which we would drape over our arms, casually throw around our necks like scarves, or let trail behind us like a bride's train.

So let me tell you the story of why we are in need of tails.

Once upon a time there were two beings, Huk and Tuk. We don't remember if they were both female, both male, or male and female. But that's immaterial. Huk and Tuk were friends — best friends — and loved doing many things together. They loved to walk in the woods. They loved to drink tea by a tiny pond in the middle of nowhere. And they loved to hold tails.

HUK and TUK

When they held tails, the rest of their body was free, free to move around independent of the other. This has great advantages, of course. You do not want to move as the other moves. Not even dancers do that.

So, while Huk or Tuk was serving tea, the other could pass the cookies. You see how this works?

Holding tails was such a great way to be together. Huk could dance up and down and Tuk could watch and tap his foot. He could feel Huk's rhythm through the connected tails. How cool is that!

They could also help each other out. If Tuk needed to reach for something far-fetched — and we all know how destabilizing that is — Huk could hold on to a tree with both arms while their tails, connected, would make sure Tuk didn't fall.

Well, there's always a sad part to a story, and so it is with this one.

Something started to happen. As humans developed tools, tails were needed less and less. Tails got shorter and shorter and eventually disappeared altogether.

So what's so sad about that?

Because the whole thing was catastrophic for the human race.

We couldn't do half the things we could before, and without tails we couldn't communicate in the way we could before, either.

See, tails could communicate with intense subtlety and accuracy.

Now, without them, we need so many, so very many, many words, and still we cannot communicate the way we used to.

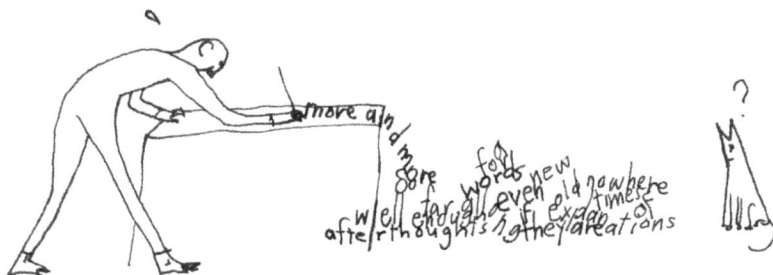

Fairy Tails

One day, Huk was trying to communicate some really subtle thing that was on his mind to Tuk, but Tuk couldn't understand.

Later, they walked in silence through the woods, not even knowing what the other was thinking or feeling.

They felt so disconnected from each other.

Then Tuk started to tell a tail — I mean tale — about dragons and lizards in faraway lands, all of whom still had tails.

And Huk understood. He started to feel connected again.

So Huk and Tuk came up with a plan.

They walked through the woods, they drank their leaf-tea, and...

they started telling tales.

These tales became what we now call fairy tales, although Huk and Tuk called them fairy tails, of course!

Tail-Theory

A very famous scientist came up with this amazing theory called string theory.

But for Huk and Tuk it is not all that amazing. After all, it was just a variation on tail-theory, really.

String theory says that everything is connected through strings. And if you think about it, tails are a kind of string.

In string theory — I mean tail-theory — everything is connected.

When everything is connected, everything has to do with everything else and every something is a part of something else. This keeps the world in balance, really. And this makes the world go around.

So how does this work then?

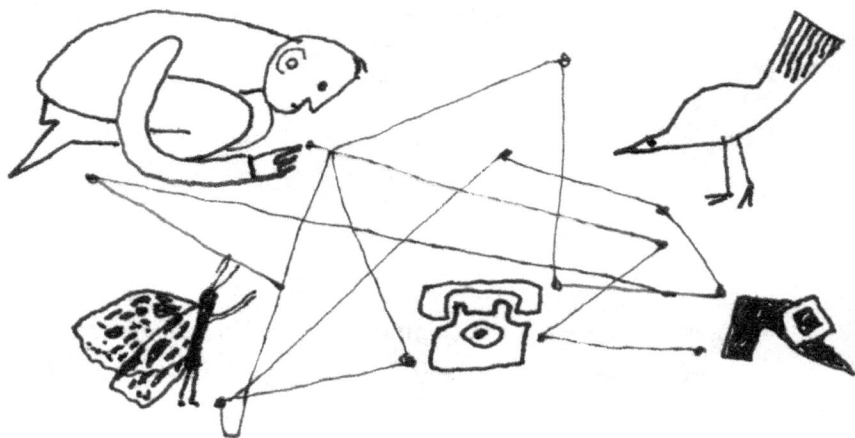

When all things are interwoven, each thing has so many different facets. That goes for humans, too.

It's almost like yin and yang, when things may be mostly so, but not entirely so, because there is also a bit of so-and-so from the other so. This sounds complicated. I think it's called zen or something like that. Zen is a misleadingly simple name for something utterly complex and incomprehensible.

But Huk and Tuk have no problem with zen. They heard these lectures, "Zen Bones" and "Zen Tales," by a guy named Alan Watts. To Huk and Tuk, zen tales — or zen tails, really — amount to the same thing.

Tails connect you and you become a part of each other; you become a yin and a yang, sort of.

But when our tails disappeared and didn't connect us to the world and others anymore, we only had ourselves to connect to.

But to be connected to yourself, you have to be connected to others. That's how the magic works.

What happened when our tails got shorter and eventually disappeared was not entirely surprising, but it was quite awful.

People became very sure of themselves, because they had nothing to contend with outside of themselves. They made their own rules and thought they applied to everyone else.

But since they were not connected to anyone anymore, what they thought and said had little worth. It didn't make them feel connected, and now they felt scared.

And so they became increasingly convinced, increasingly self-assured, so absolutist in their thinking and in their judgments, pretending to feel as grounded as they did when they were connected to everything.

That's like saying the emperor had no clothes — no tails. People didn't want to hear that. They wanted to believe they still had tails.

This was very worrisome, and Huk and Tuk were dismayed.

Huk and Tuk had decided that telling tales was a good way to reconnect, but more was needed. We needed to learn how to listen to each other in stereo-mode.

People can agree in mono-mode, but to be able to listen in stereo-mode is not easy to learn. You have your thoughts and ideas and then you have to listen and hear the other person as clearly as you hear your own voice.

It's not just His Master's Voice — remember the record label? But you have to be able to listen to your voice and that of the other, simultaneously. This starts creating a much fuller and richer sound. Yes!

When you really learn to listen, you can hear everything so clearly. Try it and you will be able to hear not a cacophony but a symphony, a symphony of life!

Knowing and Understanding

symphony

To hear a symphony instead of a cacophony, we need to connect the sounds we hear.

We have to develop a deeper understanding.

So Huk and Tuk thought about how it is that we know a lot, but do not understand a lot.

See, we can know a tree and know what it's good for, what its wood is good for and how we can use it for our benefit.

But to understand a tree is different. A tree is a million things, since it is connected to everything in

understanding a tree

the world around it — the air, the soil, the creatures that find shelter in its branches. It provides shade in the soaring heat.

A tree is not just one thing.

So to understand a tree is to apprehend the many, many things a tree really is. You cannot name them all, you cannot know them all, but you can try to understand how deeply a tree is rooted in the world and to us as well.

And roots are kind of like tails, too. Roots are like tails, because they too connect the tree to the earth and allow the tree to communicate through the earth.

And so it is with everything else that was once connected and now so often lies fragmented and forlorn, not able to be part of the warp and woof of life.

To reconnect, Huk and Tuk tell tales — I mean, tails. They practice polyphonic listening, and they work to understand the nature of things on a deeper level, below the surface of knowing.

Many knowers feel that if you cannot know something or articulate it, it is not worth much.

And maybe it is not worth much in the field of knowing, but when we move over to the field of understanding, it is worth everything in the world.

It is in understanding that we become more communal, more morally minded, more spiritual, and more emotionally intelligent.[1]

We can know a lot, but to be intelligent we also have to understand a lot.

We can have a high IQ but lack the understanding to be wise.

We can have 20/20 vision but not be perceptive. It takes understanding to be perceptive and see more than meets the eye.

We can be very successful and have a lot of money but not be able to live a life rich in meaning.

Ah! Understanding does not reside in the brain. The brain is just an organ with which we think. And we can think in very unintelligent ways, alas!

Understanding creates a much deeper (not smarter) form of intelligence.

---

1. This man named Brooks — you know, kind of like a murmuring brook — whose murmurings appear in *The New York Times* now and then, talked about this in his article "Let's Have a Better Culture War" (2016). Maybe it's better to have no war at all. That's what Huk and Tuk think, anyway.

Understanding resides in connectedness, which used to reside in our tails, but sadly those days are history.

So now we have to develop the understanding of how to become wise on our own and in our relationships with others and the world.

Trail Theory

Some of the many ways Huk and Tuk communicate now is through telling stories, through polyphonic or polylogic listening, and through understanding, not just smart-mindedness.

And there is another way to connect, too, through realizing you are a part of this miraculous universe.

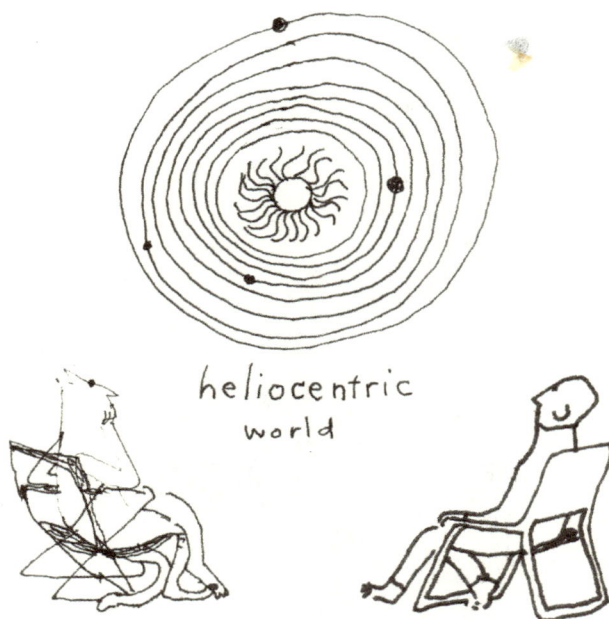

heliocentric
world

Although we know we are a part of this miraculous universe, we rarely act on our knowledge of this fact, because we lack the understanding of what this means.

See, there are trails, which are essentially paths created by tails a long, long time ago.

Creatures dragged their tails through the woods behind them and over the centuries, trails formed.

These trails are not just to make it easy for you to walk through the woods, for they also allow you to absorb the awe and wonder of the world around you and the universe even, when you look up at the shooting stars — the meteors and the trails they leave behind.

Huk and Tuk know that this view of the world helps us to see that we are not the center of the universe and never will be. Really, it's true!

We really do live in a heliocentric world, not a geocentric one!

So Huk and Tuk believe that following trails made by tails past gives us a better perspective, a deeper understanding of the universe we are a part of.

Too many who have lost their tails have also lost their ability to connect to trails past. And they are now scared.

But with a walk in the woods, following the trails of tails past, you can take in the enormity of it all, feel connected to this place called Earth, which is hurtling through space and giving you the ability to breathe and be alive!

To be alive, now that is a miracle we need to come to understand.

Tails for the "In-Between"

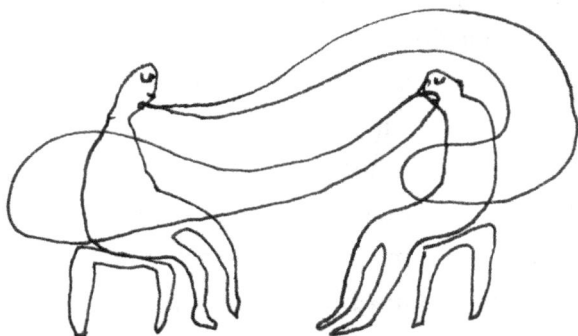

BUBER : CREATING THE "IN-BETWEEN"

Long ago there was a man named Martin Buber. He was a very wise man and devoted himself to the miracle of life.

Huk and Tuk know that tails did the work of what this man called the "in-between." In fact, tails created the "in-between."[2]

---

2. Martin Buber thought that everything started in relationship. In the beginning, there was relationship. Huk and Tuk agree, because everything is related to everything else. But there are two kinds of relationship, Buber contends. One is an I-It relationship based on utility (and leaves one feeling like less of a person) and the other is the I-Thou, which sees the other as uniquely other. When two people enter into true dialogue, they need to reach out to each other, and in doing so they create the "in-between," whereby one feels confirmed in one's whole being.

See, with tails we were connected, because the tails were a way to connect. They reached across to the other tail, something this Buber guy called the ability to "imagine the real."

Well, Huk and Tuk don't have to "imagine" anything, because it is obvious that everything was once connected through tails.

But now that we don't have any tails anymore, we need to be able to imagine things, now more than ever.

To be able to imagine something is a pretty good thing in a world caught up in the utility of everything. The problem with utility is the fact that it can be so awfully useless.

For Buber, connecting was all about dialogue, by "imagining the real," and creating the "in-between," exactly the work tails did for us before.

They helped us communicate really well together and helped us create "speech-with-meaning," another Buber thing.

Through dialogue, you feel confirmed in your whole being, as this Buber guy pointed out. In being confirmed, the You in you becomes alive and the You in the other becomes alive too!

Imagine that!

A tree without tails, or strings — or roots, really — is not alive and cannot regenerate.

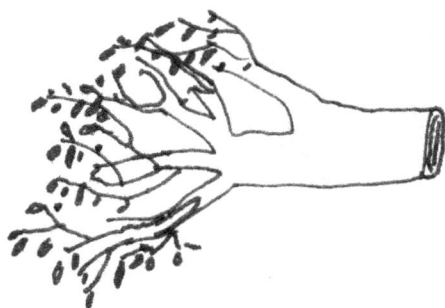

no
roots

not alive
cannot regenerate

It's the same with people. People without tails, and without connecting meaningfully to the world and other people around them, become isolated and wither away.

Speech, too, withers away and dies.

monologue

28

This happens in what Buber calls "monologue."

Without tails, without imagination, without dialogue, we have no means to regenerate.

That "in-between" thing brings about regeneration.

And Buber also warned us that only "with our whole being" can we enter into the "in-between."

Well, that makes sense, because tails, originally, were part of our whole being.

There was no such thing as tails existing separate from whole beings.

But now in this post-tail age, we can lose our whole-beingness as well. This is sad.

We become just beings to be used for the sake of another being's utility.

That's why we need to "imagine the real." We have to imagine we have tails in order to become whole again.

Postscript

In these stories, Huk and Tuk have tried to point to ways we might be able to reconnect to this beautiful world we live in and to each other.

Now we have completely different tails, visible and invisible, wires and WiFis and such.

So often they mislead rather than lead. They take us further away from where we want to be in the first place, back home. Home at home, home in the community where we live, home on this planet. Just home!

So how do we get home?

Huk and Tuk point the way back home and show how we might reconnect with where we all came from in the first place and when we all, all of us, still had tails.

Huk and Tuk point to a love of the miracle of life, a love so deep it transforms into a deep trust, knowing that you belong to this world and that you are already home!

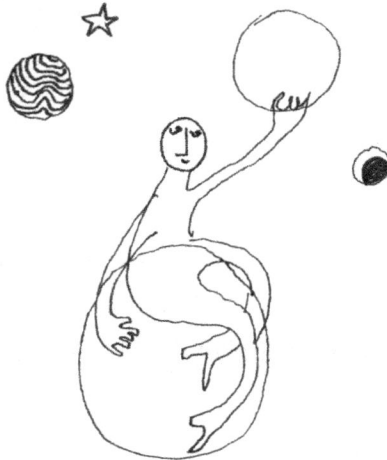

part of the
universe

References

Brooks, David. "Let's Have a Better Culture War."
The New York Times, June 7, 2016.

Buber, Martin. *I and Thou*. Translated by Ronald Gregor
Smith. New York: Charles Scribner's Sons, 1958.

Friedman, Maurice. *Martin Buber: The Life of Dialogue*.
Chicago: The University of Chicago Press, 1976.

Watts, Alan. "Zen Bones." *Eastern Wisdom Collection*.
Lecture available at www.alanwatts.org/audio/
Zen Bones: https://youtu.be/we_Cv2v8P4M
Zen Tales: https://youtu.be/54mkP1DJLDs

Maria deVenza Tillmanns

Maria teaches a "Philosophy with Children" program in underserved San Diego schools in partnership with the University of California, San Diego. In 1980, she attended Dr. Matthew Lipman's workshop on philosophy for children and later wrote her dissertation on philosophical counseling and teaching under the direction of Martin Buber scholar Dr. Maurice Friedman. She has publications in a number of international journals. For Maria, philosophy is an art form, and she enjoys painting with ideas. Philosophy has helped her navigate the world in all its complexity, including having a multicultural background and having been raised in the US as well as in the Netherlands. She came back to the US to study and moved across the Atlantic multiple times.

Blair Thornley

Blair Thornley is an award-winning illustrator living in San Diego and Truro, Cape Cod. Among her extensive client list are *The New York Times, Boston Globe, Washington Post, L A Times, Vogue, Vanity Fair*, Herman Miller, and Neiman Marcus. She created the cover illustrations for a reprinted series of Peter De Vries's books, and was a contributor to the recently published *Collected Fables* by James Thurber. Thornley's work is shown regularly at Harmon Gallery in Wellfleet, Massachusetts and has been exhibited at Judy Saslow Gallery in Chicago, Pasadena Museum of California Art, and at the Society of Illustrators in New York.

www.ingramcontent.com/pod-product-compliance
Lightning Source LLC
Chambersburg PA
CBHW031635040426
42452CB00007B/843